Seashore to Spot

Illustrated by Stephanie Fizer Coleman

Designed by Lenka Hrehova and Jenny Brown
Words by Sam Smith

You can use the stickers to fill in the chart
at the back of the book, so you can keep
track of the seashore life you have seen.

Rock pools

Look for the thin blue line around the base

Beadlet anemone

This anemone's body is usually red or green, with a bright blue 'bead' under each tentacle.

Common hermit crab

Doesn't have its own shell, so it finds empty ones to live in. Try looking for it in whelk and cockle shells.

Sea oak

It has fronds like bright red oak leaves. You can often find it growing on the stalks of large, brown seaweeds.

Toad crab

Look for this crab's pear-shaped shell, which is often covered with sponges and seaweed.

Often found caught in lobster pots

Thornback spider crab

You might find this long-legged crab amongst oarweed. It can be easily recognized by its spiny, oval shell.

Gut laver

Also called gutweed. Its tube-like fronds are inflated like balloons. Look for it covering the surface of pools higher up the shore.

Tide pools

Feeds on acorn barnacles

Montagu's blenny

Look for the fleshy crest between this fish's eyes, and the pale blue spots on its brown body.

Butterfish

You might spot this fish hiding under stones and seaweed. Its slippery body is flattened sideways.

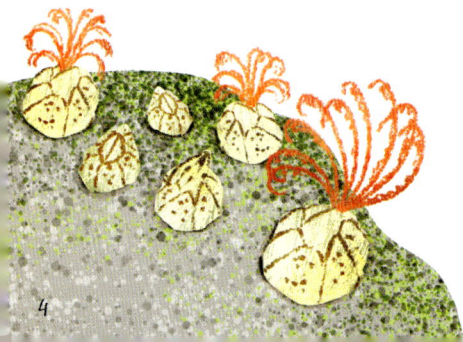

Acorn barnacle

You'll see these on the rocks of any shore. When underwater, its legs come out to catch food that drifts past.

Common starfish

Has five arms with bumpy spines.
You can often find them in shallow
water or washed up on the shore.

Colour varies from orange to green or grey

Cushion star

Look for this small, thick
starfish tucked into crevices
or under rocks.

Common octopus

Lives in shallow water
amongst rocks, but can be
hard to spot as it changes
colour to blend in.

Rocky shores

Shore rockling

Try spotting this long, brown fish under stones and seaweed. It uses its three whisker-like barbels to find food.

Its fins can be seen moving in a continuous wave motion

Rock goby

You can see rock gobies clinging to rocks during the summer months so they don't get swept away.

Females may be seen carrying orange eggs on their belly

Shore crab

Look for this common crab in shallow water on any shore. Its spiked shell is normally green, but may be orange.

Common limpet

Found clamped to rocks on all coasts with its muscular foot. When the tide is in, it crawls around eating algae.

Common brittlestar

Can be seen under stones in shallow water and rock pools. Its long arms are very fragile, so don't touch them.

Eats fish, crabs and squid

Grey seal

Varies from black with white spots to white with black spots. Look for it resting on land at low tide and sunset.

Rocky coasts

Edible sea urchin

This sea urchin is noticeable by its large size and its reddish spines, which drop off when it dies.

Its shell is called a test

Knotted wrack

You can spot this seaweed growing in dense masses on sheltered shores. Small air bladders keep it upright in the water.

Snakelocks anemone

Look for it attached to rocks in shallow water, but watch out – its snakelike tentacles can give you a nasty sting.

Irish moss

Commonly seen on rocks on
most coasts and in estuaries.
Varies from green to purple,
and can appear bright
blue underwater.

Common mussel

Mussels live in large groups on many
coasts, anchoring themselves to rocks
and each other with sticky threads.

Dog whelk

You'll find this sea snail wherever
there are mussels and barnacles,
whose shells it bores through
to feed on them.

Shell colour can vary sometimes
depending on the food it eats

Sandy shores

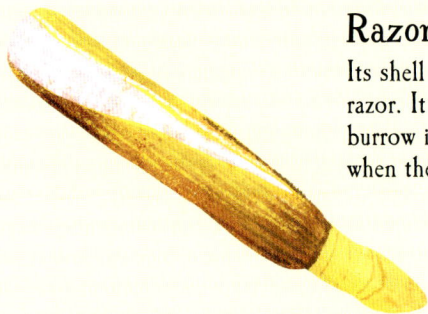

Razor shell
Its shell looks like an old-fashioned razor. It uses its muscular foot to burrow into the sand or mud when the tide goes out.

Common cockle
Look for cockles buried in the sand on the lower beach. Their ribbed shells can be off-white, yellow or brown.

Flowers in July and August

Sea centaury
You might spot this plant growing low to the ground in sandy places near the sea.

Sea bindweed

This plant's shiny, heart-shaped leaves can be seen sprawling over the ground on sand dunes on most coasts.

Flowers June to September

Edible crab

Look under boulders and in shallow water for this brown crab's oval shell and black-tipped claws.

Shelduck

This large duck likes sandy and muddy coasts. Watch for its slow-beating wings in flight.

11

Shingle beaches

Rayed trough shell

Look on gravelly or sandy shores. It has pale rays stretching across it, and is light purple inside.

Common whelk

This huge sea snail is found in shallow water and can measure the width of this book. The empty shells are often used by hermit crabs.

Tiny blue flowers attract a variety of butterflies

Sea holly

Can be seen on sandy beaches too. Look for its silver-green, prickly leaves. Flowers from July to September.

Yellow horned poppy

You can spot clumps of this plant growing on stony shores, sand dunes and cliffs. In summer, its long seed pod looks like a horn.

Little tern

This small seabird is a summer visitor that nests in small groups on pebbly beaches.

Dives into the water from the air to catch fish

Ringed plover

You might see this short wading bird running along the shore in stops and starts, and tilting over to feed.

Shallow water

Plumose anemone

Look for this anemone just below the water on pier supports. Its fine, dense tentacles make it appear fluffy.

Plocamium

You can spot this distinctive red, feathery-tipped seaweed in shallow water, or washed ashore.

Finger-like segments are called digits

Oarweed

Found on rocks in shallow water, this brown, leathery seaweed has a wide, hand-like blade, split into flat strips.

Sea fan

This pale pink coral may be seen on rocks below the surface, or washed up on the beach.

Common sunstar

This large, beautifully patterned starfish has up to 15 arms. It lives on the seabed near to the shore.

Common prawn

Look closely in shallow water and rock pools. It has long feelers, but its body is nearly transparent.

Some have bright blue and yellow markings on their legs

Coastal waters

Harbour porpoise

You might see one, or a small group, near headlands. Listen for the loud "chuff" as it surfaces to breathe.

Moon jellyfish

Transparent with a purple rim and four crescents on top. Common on all coasts, and harmless. Often seen washed up on beaches.

Be careful not to step on its venomous spines

Weever

This small fish is a clumsy swimmer, and can be found buried in the sand in shallow water.

Sand smelt

Look for these in large groups near the surface. They are pale, silvery-yellow with a dark stripe on one side.

Has a large triangular back fin, and a bulbous snout

Basking shark

You might spot this gentle giant in the ocean in summer. Look for it from above when you're high up on cliffs.

Sometimes known as a brain sponge

Sea orange

This large, round sponge can be orange, yellow or white. Look for it attached to rocks or shells in shallow water.

Estuaries

Breaks open shellfish with its strong beak

Oystercatcher

Listen for this black and white
wading bird's "peep"-ing call
as it hunts for shellfish.

Common oyster

The two halves of its scaly shell
are different shapes, and pearly
white inside. Look for them
in shallow water.

Fast swimmer, and dives
for 20-30 minutes

Common seal

You might see these spotted
seals out of the water on
sandbanks and sheltered shores.

Sea wormwood

Look for this strong-smelling plant growing above the tide level. Its grey-green leaves are covered in a soft down.

Brownish or yellowish flowers in August and September

Sand shrimp

You can often find this shrimp in the sand and mud. It has broad, flattened claws on its front legs.

Swims well with long, thick tail and webbed feet

Otter

More common in fresh water, but you can sometimes spot them in or near the sea. Mostly active at night.

Cliffs

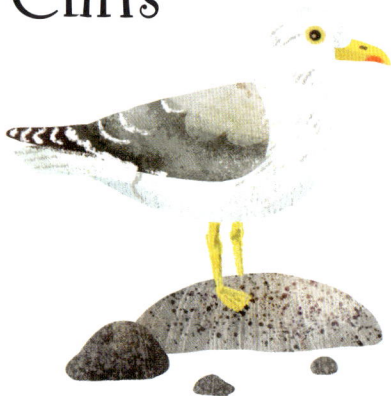

Herring gull

Look for the red patch on this large, noisy gull's beak. Nests on cliffs, and easy to spot on all coasts.

Thrift

Also called sea pink. Grows in thick, cushiony tufts on rock faces near the sea. Flowers March to September.

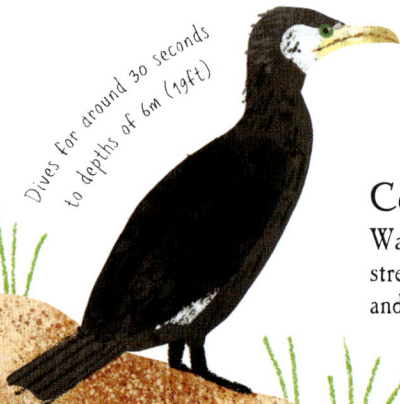

Dives for around 30 seconds to depths of 6m (19ft)

Cormorant

Watch for cormorants on rocks stretching out their wings to dry, and spot the white face patch.

Golden samphire

You can find clumps of this shiny-leaved plant growing on cliffs, shingle and saltmarshes. Large yellow flowers July to August.

Sheds colourful outer parts of beak after breeding season

Puffin

This plump seabird with a multicoloured beak can be seen in April to August, nesting on northern rock faces.

Viper's bugloss

Look for this plant's bristly stems and long, rough leaves on clifftops and sand dunes. The blue flowers grow from pink buds in June to September.

Spotting chart

Once you've spotted some seashore life from this book, find its sticker at the back, and stick it on this chart in the space below its name.

Acorn barnacle	Basking shark	Beadlet anemone	Butterfish	Common brittlestar
Common cockle	Common hermit crab	Common limpet	Common mussel	Common octopus
Common oyster	Common prawn	Common seal	Common starfish	Common sunstar
Common whelk	Cormorant	Cushion star	Dog whelk	Edible crab
Edible sea urchin	Golden samphire	Grey seal	Gut laver	Harbour porpoise

Herring gull	Irish moss	Knotted wrack	Little tern	Montagu's blenny
Moon jellyfish	Oarweed	Otter	Oystercatcher	Plocamium
Plumose anemone	Puffin	Rayed trough shell	Razor shell	Ringed plover
Rock goby	Sand shrimp	Sand smelt	Sea bindweed	Sea centaury
Sea fan	Sea holly	Sea oak	Sea orange	Sea wormwood
Shelduck	Shore crab	Shore rockling	Snakelocks anemone	Thornback spider crab
Thrift	Toad crab	Viper's bugloss	Weever	Yellow horned poppy

Index

First published in 2021 by Usborne Publishing Ltd., Usborne House, 83-85 Saffron Hill, London EC1N 8RT, England.
usborne.com Copyright © 2021 Usborne Publishing Ltd. The name Usborne and the Balloon logo are Trade Marks
of Usborne Publishing Ltd. All rights reserved. No part of this publication may be reproduced, stored in a
retrieval system or transmitted in any form or by any means, electronic, mechanical, photocopying,
recording or otherwise without the prior permission of the publisher. Printed in China. UKE.